The
Northeast

Heather E. Schwartz

Consultants

Brian Allman
Principal
Upshur County Schools, West Virginia

James D. Zimmer Jr., M.A., M.S.Ed.
Instructional Coordinator for Social Studies
Cecil County Public Schools, Maryland

Krista Provost, M.Ed.
Social Studies Teacher
West Milford Township Public Schools, New Jersey

Robert L. Callamari, M.Ed.
American History Teacher
West Milford School District, New Jersey

Publishing Credits

Rachelle Cracchiolo, M.S.Ed., *Publisher*
Emily R. Smith, M.A.Ed., *SVP of Content Development*
Véronique Bos, *VP of Creative*
Dona Herweck Rice, *Senior Content Manager*
Dani Neiley, *Editor*
Fabiola Sepulveda, *Series Graphic Designer*

Image Credits: p8 ZUMA Press, Inc. / Alamy Stock Photo; p11 Associated Press; p12 Library of Congress [LC-DIG-pga-09270]; p13 (left) Shutterstock/Luciano Mortula - LGM; p13 (right) GL Archive / Alamy Stock Photo; p15 NPS/Tim Ertel; 15 (bottom) New York Public Library Digital Collection; p17 (top) National Portrait Gallery; p17 (bottom) Library of Congress [LC-DIG-ppmsca-53264]; p18 (left) Shutterstock/Maverick Pictures; p18 (right) Chris Fitzgerald/CandidatePhotos/Newscom; p19 (top) Declaration of Independence, 181; p19 (bottom) Science History Images / Alamy Stock Photo; p22 North Wind Picture Archives / Alamy Stock Photo; p23 (top) Sarin Images / GRANGER; p24 Sarin Images / GRANGER ; all other images from iStock and/or Shutterstock

Library of Congress Cataloging-in-Publication Data

Names: Schwartz, Heather E., author.
Title: The Northeast / Heather E. Schwartz.
Description: Huntington Beach, CA : Teacher Created Materials, [2023] |
    Includes index. | Audience: Grades 4-6 | Summary: "When you are in the
    Northeast, there is no mistaking your location. It is a unique area of
    the United States. Learn how history, cuisine, and culture set this
    region apart from the rest of the country"-- Provided by publisher.
Identifiers: LCCN 2022021231 (print) | LCCN 2022021232 (ebook) | ISBN
    9781087690988 (paperback) | ISBN 9781087691145 (ebook)
Subjects: LCSH: New England--Juvenile literature. | Middle Atlantic
    States--Juvenile literature.
Classification: LCC F4.3 .S39 2023 (print) | LCC F4.3 (ebook) | DDC
    974--dc23/eng/20220506
LC record available at https://lccn.loc.gov/2022021231
LC ebook record available at https://lccn.loc.gov/2022021232

**Shown on the cover is Portland Head Light in
Cape Elizabeth, Maine.**

TCM | Teacher Created Materials

5482 Argosy Avenue
Huntington Beach, CA 92649
www.tcmpub.com
ISBN 978-1-0876-9098-8

Table of Contents

Piece of the Puzzle

A map of the United States looks like a puzzle, with each piece a different state. But the country is also made up of regions. The Northeast, as you might guess, is the name for the northeastern part of the country.

Part of what makes each region unique is its location. But there is much more to it than that. Each region has its own geography, weather, and seasonal changes. Each has its own history. The **culture**, civics, and economics of each region differ, too.

If you were traveling across the United States without a GPS, a map, or even road signs, you would probably be able to tell when you reached the Northeast. How? Scents, sights, and sounds offer clues. You might smell the ocean, see a famous landmark, or hear a particular accent. You might sample a dish you cannot get anywhere else in the country— or the world.

There are many ways to know you are in the Northeast. It is unlike any other region of the United States.

Delaware seaside

Mount Washington, New Hampshire

Lancaster, Pennsylvania

Northeastern Geography

It can be easy to tell where one state ends and another begins. If you are traveling, you will cross a border. On major roads, you will usually see a sign welcoming you into the next state.

The Northeast region has borders, too. To the north, the region ends at Canada. To the south, it stops at West Virginia and Virginia. On the west, it borders Ohio. On the east, it borders the Atlantic Ocean.

In this book, 11 states are included in the Northeastern region. They are some of the oldest states in the country. Many of them are quite small in terms of area, although their populations may be large. The states are Connecticut, Delaware, Maine, Maryland, Massachusetts, New Hampshire, New Jersey, New York, Pennsylvania, Rhode Island, and Vermont.

Much of the land in the Northeast is forest. Many people come to the area to see the colorful changing of seasons among the trees. But each state does not look exactly the same. You will find rocky beaches in Maine. There are fields of farmland in Pennsylvania. New York is home to the world-famous Niagara Falls and the country's largest **urban** area, New York City.

The Northeast is famous for its mountains, too. The nation's windiest spot is Mount Washington in New Hampshire. Some of the oldest mountains in the world can be found in Pennsylvania and Maryland. The Blue Ridge Mountains of the Appalachian range are more than one billion years old!

The Northeast

Maine

Vermont

New Hampshire

New York

Massachusetts

Rhode Island

Connecticut

Pennsylvania

New Jersey

Delaware

Maryland

New England

Six states in the Northeast make up the area known as New England. This is the region first settled by colonists from England. Explorer John Smith called the area New England in 1616. The states of New England are Connecticut, Maine, Massachusetts, New Hampshire, Rhode Island, and Vermont.

Native Peoples of the Northeast

The first people of the Northeast lived there for thousands of years before others came to explore and settle the area. Most of the history in recorded time belongs to the native peoples.

The native peoples of the Northeast belonged to many cultures. Their communities were called **tribes**. Major tribes of the region included the Abenaki, Cayuga, Delaware, Iroquois, Micmac, Pequot, and Wampanoag. Many of these tribes still exist, making their cultures some of the longest-lived ones in the world. Within each tribe, there were also smaller **clans**. Clans were often named for animals, such as Bear, Heron, Snipe, Turtle, and Wolf.

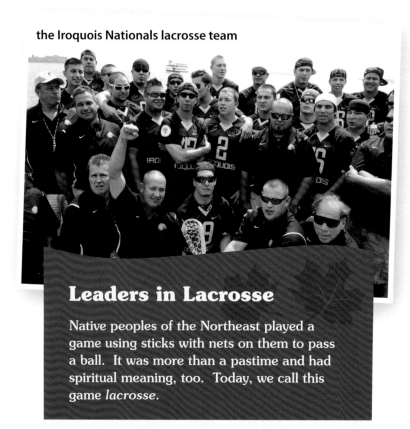

the Iroquois Nationals lacrosse team

Leaders in Lacrosse

Native peoples of the Northeast played a game using sticks with nets on them to pass a ball. It was more than a pastime and had spiritual meaning, too. Today, we call this game *lacrosse*.

Much of the history of the tribes is known through oral tradition. That is the passing down of stories as they are told to new generations. But some of the people also wrote their stories on scrolls. The scrolls were made from the bark of birch trees. The native peoples took great care **inscribing** the birchbark scrolls and preserving them. They also made copies of the scrolls over time to ensure that they could be read by future generations. Some of these old scrolls can be seen in modern museums.

There were three language families among the peoples of the Northeast. Some different tribes shared a common language. The Algonquian language group was the most widespread of all.

The people of the tribes mainly hunted for their food. Game was plentiful in and around the forests, meadows, and rivers of the region. Seafood was ample along the Atlantic coast and its many **inlets**. As hunters, they often moved to follow food sources. But permanent villages were common as well. Either way, communities worked together for their food, shelter, and other needs.

American Indian Life Today

In the Northeast, there are 18 American Indian **reservations**. There are 16 different tribes. These tribes live in New York, Maine, Connecticut, Massachusetts, and Rhode Island. They include the Maliseet, Oneida, Penobscot, Seneca, and many more. Of course, many American Indians live away from reservations as well. They live and work in towns and cities across the region.

Many American Indians of today work hard to preserve their cultures and traditions. They care for the land where they live. They watch over endangered animals that share their environments. For example, the Maliseet people are known for protecting bald eagles. The Penobscot people protect Atlantic salmon. The National Native American Program is an agency within the U.S. Fish and Wildlife Service. It works with tribal nations to protect the land and wildlife that is important to them.

Symbol of Respect

Bald eagles are a symbol of the United States. But only American Indians are allowed to possess their feathers. The law was passed to respect the tribes' cultural and religious use of the feathers.

The people of many Northeastern tribes honor their traditional cultures with powwows. These gatherings bring people together from wherever they live. Traditional food, songs, dance, stories, and clothing are important parts of powwows. Goods and crafts are often sold there. But everything at a powwow is not just part of old traditions. Modern culture is there as well.

While many native peoples remember and honor traditions, their lives today are like most other Americans. They work, go to school, play sports, watch television, eat pizza, and live typical modern lives. American Indians today honor the past but live in the present as people everywhere do.

Mashpee Wampanoag tribe members play their traditional drums.

Colonies to Country

Beginning in the early 15th century, people from Europe began to explore the world in search of wealth, knowledge, and new trade routes. First explorers and then **settlers** came to American shores.

The Northeast was one of the first regions of the future United States to be settled by Europeans. In this region, the people came mainly from England. The English people settled the area as **colonies** of Great Britain. They were seeking a new land of opportunity. Some people wanted more religious freedom. Others wanted a chance for a better life.

When they sailed across the Atlantic Ocean, the people left their old lives behind forever. They knew they would not return to their homes. The journey was too far and too dangerous. Once they arrived, the settlers formed their own communities. They lived separately from the native peoples. The settlers worked as farmers. They fished and hunted as well.

Pilgrims of the *Mayflower* arrive in Massachusetts.

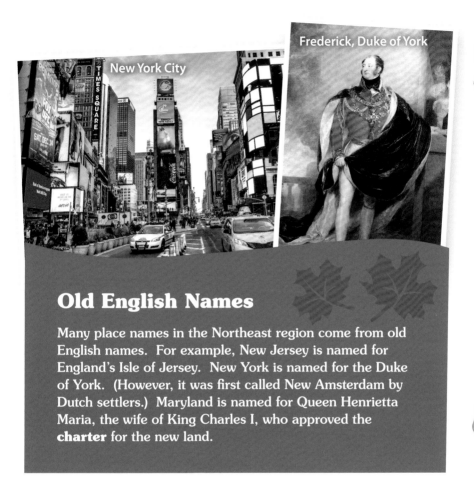

New York City

Frederick, Duke of York

Old English Names

Many place names in the Northeast region come from old English names. For example, New Jersey is named for England's Isle of Jersey. New York is named for the Duke of York. (However, it was first called New Amsterdam by Dutch settlers.) Maryland is named for Queen Henrietta Maria, the wife of King Charles I, who approved the **charter** for the new land.

The first settlers came to the Northeast on a ship called the *Mayflower*. Its 102 passengers did not intend to wind up where they did. They were aiming for Virginia, but a storm sent them off course. In 1620, they landed in Massachusetts and founded Plymouth Colony. These people were later known as the Pilgrims.

In the years that followed, more settlers came. They set up more colonies. Many of these colonies were in the Northeast. America won freedom from Britain in 1776. The early colonies became some of the nation's first states.

The Heart of the Nation

People living in the country's first colonies had to set up new communities. They needed schools and systems of government. Many of their ideas were born in the Northeast. Harvard University was founded in 1636. It is the country's oldest college. This highly esteemed school is still open in Massachusetts.

The Northeast region has a big influence on much of the United States today. That has a lot to do with some of the major cities found there. Manhattan, in New York City, is the financial center of the United States. It is also an important financial center in the world. Much of the U.S. **economy** is centered in New York.

Baltimore was one of the top three points of entry for **immigrants** into the United States. (The first was Ellis Island in New York.) The first commercial railroad in the country was started in Baltimore. The country's national anthem, "The Star-Spangled Banner," was written just outside Baltimore as well.

Philadelphia is the second-largest city on the East Coast and the sixth-largest in the country. It played a very important role in shaping the United States. The Liberty Bell, a symbol of American freedom, makes its home in Philadelphia.

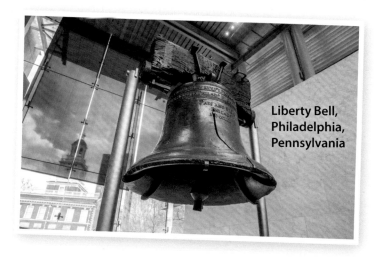

Liberty Bell, Philadelphia, Pennsylvania

Fort McHenry, Baltimore, Maryland

Pennsylvania Evening Post, 1776

Philadelphia Firsts

Philadelphia is a city of famous firsts. The country's first daily newspaper was in Philadelphia. It was home to the first hospital and first medical school in the country as well. It also had the first U.S. zoo.

Northeastern Mindset

Throughout history, big events forced people to choose a side. During the American Revolution, Patriots wanted freedom. Loyalists took the side of the king of England. Most people in the Northeast wanted freedom, too. They fought for that freedom. They helped pave the way for a new nation. The ideas of freedom and liberty have remained important to the people of the Northeast since that time.

Later, the Civil War tore the country apart. The Union wanted to end slavery but keep the country together. The Confederacy wanted to break away. They wanted to keep slavery legal. The Northeast fought for the Union. The region helped win the war and end slavery.

"Live Free or Die"

New Hampshire has a state motto: "Live Free or Die." It comes from a letter written by General John Stark in 1809. He was a state war hero who led troops during the French and Indian War and the Revolutionary War.

W. E. B. Du Bois

Over hundreds of years, people in the Northeast have developed attitudes and traits that define the region. Northeasterners are often described as resilient. Some people say they are relaxed and creative. Many great American writers come from the region. Louisa May Alcott, James Baldwin, Robert Frost, W. E. B. Du Bois, Emily Dickinson, and Stephen King are just some of them.

Louisa May Alcott

Education matters to the people of the Northeast, as there are many colleges and universities throughout the Northeast. In fact, there are about 35 colleges and universities in Boston alone! The famous group of eight colleges known as the Ivy League is all in the Northeast. These schools are known for their tough classes and academic excellence.

Princeton University, New Jersey

Civics

Throughout history, the people of the Northeast have been known for their civic involvement. The idea for town hall meetings started in the Northeast. People during colonial days met to discuss public business in their town halls. Most communities had such a building. Meetings like these are held to this day throughout the Northeast. They are a common part of civic life. Town leaders may be in attendance or run the meetings. But the people use the meetings to have a say in their governments.

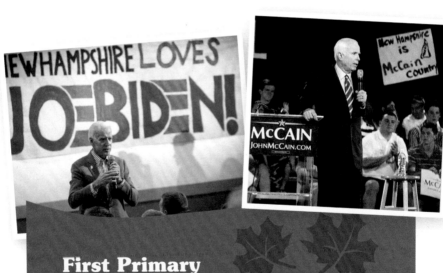

First Primary

Every four years, there are primary elections throughout the United States. The presidential candidate for each major party is decided in the primaries. The first primary each year is usually in New Hampshire. The state is small and does not have many votes overall. But its role as the first to hold a primary gets a lot of attention each year and can influence voting across the country.

Iroquois Confederacy leaders

Some of the big ideas at the heart of the United States also came from the Northeast region. More specifically, they came from the native peoples who lived there before the colonists arrived. The Iroquois Confederacy had a system of government that was based on **democratic** ideas. It showed how nations could live together peacefully. U.S. Founders were impressed with these ideas. They used some of them as they developed the new U.S. Constitution and system of government.

Many Founders were also from the Northeast region, and the Northeast played an important role in the country's foundation. Before the start of the American Revolution, **delegates** met in Philadelphia. The Declaration of Independence was written in this city as well. New York City was the U.S. capital when the U.S. Constitution became law.

Life in the Northeast

The Northeast has a culture all its own. Life there is different from life in other parts of the United States. Why? It comes from the region's location as well as the people who live there.

The population is **diverse**. People from all over the world live in the Northeast and make it their home.

The **cuisine** is diverse, too. Coastal states have plenty of seafood, such as lobster and crab. The region is also known for classic foods such as Boston baked beans, New England clam chowder, and Philly cheesesteaks. Food critics have said that some of the best restaurants in the world can be found in major cities such as New York, Boston, and Philadelphia.

Dramatic seasonal changes are also a big part of life in the Northeast. In some regions, one season slides gently into the next. But in the Northeast, the changes can be startling. Summers are usually green and vibrant but also hot and humid. Winters can be very cold and even harsh with snowstorms and freezing rains. Spring may also be chilly and wet, but it is also filled with signs of life popping up through the melting snow. New plants and flowers grow everywhere. But perhaps most popular of all in the Northeast is fall. When the leaves turn bright red, yellow, and orange, people flock to see them. Northeast autumns draw tourists from around the world.

Better Than PB&J

Take two slices of bread, spread with peanut butter and marshmallow, and you have one of Massachusetts's most famous sandwiches: the fluffernutter. Fans love it so much that they have tried for years to make it the official state sandwich.

lobster fisherman

Montpelier, Vermont

clam chowder

21

Business and Economics

In the late 1700s, textile mills began opening in the Northeast. Many people found jobs in these factories. They produced cloth. The first textile mill opened in Rhode Island. Soon, many more opened throughout the region. Lowell, Massachusetts, was famous for its factories. The factories hired young women as workers. They offered women a chance to live and work independently.

Industry grew in the Northeast after the War of 1812. It was still going strong as the country headed into the Civil War. Northern states produced leather, firearms, iron, and many other goods. Jobs in industry were on the rise. By 1860, only about 40 percent of people in the North worked on farms. But their output increased thanks to the use of machines on their land. The machines helped them produce more crops. They could even leave their land in the care of others while they fought in the Civil War.

For many years, the economy in the North was built on manufacturing and selling goods. People had dependable jobs. They earned decent wages. They had money to spend. These factors created the region's economy. The Northeast was **prosperous**.

Mill workers use industrial textile machines in the 1800s.

farming machine of the 1800s

Lowell Mill Girls

The women who came to Lowell to work were called "Lowell mill girls." They were young and new to the city. While there, they organized protests and strikes to fight against poor working conditions.

A New Beginning

After World War II, the jobs in the Northeast began to change. Industry moved out of the region to other areas. It was cheaper to make goods in other states and other countries. That was good for businesses but bad for workers. Many people lost their factory jobs. Sometimes, whole towns suffered.

Other businesses came into the Northeast when factories left. These new businesses focused on work in finance, technology, education, and medicine. These jobs changed the population of the region. Workers used to move there for factory jobs. Skilled workers still can find jobs in communications there. They can work in **microelectronics**, computers, and **biotechnology**. They come to the region from all over the world.

New York Stock Exchange in 1800

Measuring the Region's Economy

Gross domestic product (GDP) is a measurement of the total value of goods and services in an area during a specific time. In 2020, the New York City area had a GDP of about $1.5 trillion.

Johns Hopkins Hospital, Baltimore, Maryland

One of the major industries in the Northeast is health care. Leading medical research centers, hospitals, and schools are found throughout the region. It is said that one out of every six doctors in the United States is trained in Philadelphia. The Johns Hopkins Hospital (Baltimore) and Mount Sinai Hospital (New York) are known throughout the world.

Merging History

History in the Northeast runs deep. Native peoples lived on and with the land for thousands of years. Then, a new nation found its foothold and became the United States. Much of the early history of the nation lies in the Northeast.

Wherever you go throughout the Northeast, you will find signs of this history. Markers on buildings proudly call out their past importance. Road signs point out battlefields and historic sites. Place names tell of the people, places, and events that came before. Old European names are commonly found. But also, many American Indian words designate places and show their importance in history. Places such as Mohawk Mountain, Kennebec River, Hyannis, Connecticut, and thousands more are based in native words. History is in the names themselves.

Old and new history merge throughout the Northeast. And the people of the Northeast celebrate and honor it all. All the phases of history have brought the Northeast to where it is today. It is a thriving, diverse, and important region. It plays a major role in the life of the United States.

Imagine visiting the Northeast today. You might head out for a hike in a quiet forest filled with pine trees. You could just as easily visit one of the region's vibrant cities. Either way, you would see a region that is healthy, unique, and ready for whatever comes next!

Augusta, Maine

Early Risers

As the easternmost state in the United States, Maine is the site of the country's earliest sunrise. It attracts millions of tourists to Cadillac Mountain and Mars Hill every year.

Mount Washington Summit, New Hampshire

Map It!

The Northeast includes large cities, farmland, and suburban areas. Each offers different sights to see and explore. Maybe you would like to visit some of them yourself. It is a great way to learn about local history, try new foods, and experience activities that make the Northeast so much fun.

Pretend you are promoting the region to tourists. Make a map to show them the region's many attractions.

1. Draw a map of the region, showing all state boundaries.
2. Add major rivers, mountains, and other land features.
3. Highlight the interesting landmarks of the region, such as Niagara Falls, New York City, and Mount Washington.
4. Research to discover more about the region. Include at least one landmark from each state in the Northeast.
5. After you finish your map, write a sentence about each landmark. Tell what it is and why it is worth visiting.

covered bridge spanning the Housatonic River, Connecticut

Taughannock Falls, New York

Glossary

biotechnology—the use of living cells to make useful products

charter—a document that declares that a community has been officially established

clans—large groups of people who form a community

colonies—areas that are controlled by or belong to a distant country

cuisine—a style of cooking food in a particular way

culture—the beliefs, customs, arts, etc. of a particular society, group, place, or time

delegates—people who are chosen or elected to vote or act for others

democratic—relating to a form of government in which the people vote for leaders

diverse—made up of people or things that are different from one another

economy—the system of making, selling, and buying goods and services in a particular place

immigrants—people who come to a country to live there

inlets—small arms of large bodies of water that cut into the land, such as small bays or creeks

inscribing—adding words to

microelectronics—the design, production, or use of very small electronic devices and circuits

prosperous—having success, usually by making money

reservations—areas of land set aside for American Indian tribes

settlers—people who go to live in a new place where usually there are few or no people

tribes—groups of people that include many families and relatives who have the same language, customs, and beliefs

urban—of or relating to cities

Index

Learn More!

General John Stark was a war hero from New Hampshire. He led troops in two famous battles of the American Revolution in nearby states.

- Research to find out what happened in each battle and what General Stark did.

- Create a poster that shows where and when those battles took place.

- Include pictures on your poster.

- Be sure to include who fought in each battle and who won.

Meredith, New Hampshire